Laugh Lines

for

Educators

Laugh Lines

for
Educators

Diane Hodges

CORWIN PRESS
A SAGE Publications Company
Thousand Oaks, California

For information:

Corwin Press
A Sage Publications Company
2455 Teller Road
Thousand Oaks, California 91320
www.corwinpress.com

Sage Publications Ltd.
1 Oliver's Yard
55 City Road
London, EC1Y 1SP
United Kingdom

Sage Publications India Pvt. Ltd.
B–42, Panchsheel Enclave
Post Box 4109
New Delhi 110 017 India

Printed in the United States of America

A catalog record of this book is available from the Library of Congress.

ISBN 1–4129–2674–2 (cloth)
ISBN 1–4129–2675–0 (pbk.)

This book is printed on acid–free paper.

06   07   08   09   10   9   8   7   6   5   4   3   2

Acquisitions Editor:	Elizabeth Brenkus
Editorial Assistants:	Candice L. Ling and Desirée Enayati
Production Editor:	Laureen Shea
Proofreader:	Colleen Brennan
Cover Designer:	Rose Storey

contents

Where do jokes come from? Who knows? There are some really talented people somewhere out there who think these up. I hope you will duplicate the pages and use them within your work setting.

This book started as "Restroom Readings." When I was Director of a school, I wanted to include humor and motivational sayings in documents I sent to the staff. I included this type of material in memos and put them on the bulletin board, but I was never convinced that they actually reached the staff. One day I realized that a place all staff members frequent is the staff restroom. Periodically, I put cartoons and sayings on the wall in the restroom (or in the stalls). Soon others were making their own contributions to "The Wall." At the end of the year, I had the messages duplicated into booklet form and gave copies to staff.

The book also makes a great gift for friends and family who are ill. Humor just helps you feel better!

— *Diane Hodges*

Find humor in all aspects of your life. . . .
It is then that you will be able to survive it.

about the author

Diane Hodges is the Managing Partner of Threshold Group, a consulting firm specializing in training and staff development. After thirty years as an educator, Diane is delighting audiences nationwide with her acclaimed presentation series for educational administrators and staff.

She is the author of *Looking Forward to Monday Morning* in which she has compiled ideas for recognition, appreciation, and fun things that can be done at work—all on a low budget. It shows how to have fun during staff meetings, lunch time, and holidays and how to make each day a FUNday.

She is one of the foremost authorities on high school and professional portfolios as well as other "sales" tools and "leave behinds" that help in the application and interview process. She has captured these ideas in *Your Portfolio: Your Passport to HIRE and HIGHER Education* and *Your Portfolio: A Visual Résumé*.

She has served as a human resources director, director of instructional services, executive director of career and technology education, principal, counselor, and instructor. She earned her doctorate from Michigan State University, has received twelve national and state leadership awards, and is the author of six books. Diane lives in San Diego, CA, and loves every minute of the weather!

You make me laugh. . . .
You make me smile. . . .
You are my best friend.

children

God's Children

After creating Heaven and Earth, God created Adam and Eve. And the first thing he said was "Don't!"

"Don't what?" Adam replied.

"Don't eat the forbidden fruit," God said.

"Forbidden fruit? We have forbidden fruit? Hey, Eve . . . we have forbidden fruit!"

"No way!"

"Yes, way!!"

"Do NOT eat the fruit!" said God.

"Why?"

"Because I am your Father and I said so!" God replied (wondering why He hadn't stopped creation after making the elephants). A few minutes later, God saw His children having an apple break, and was He upset!

"Didn't I tell you not to eat the fruit?" God, as our first parent, asked.

"Uh huh," Adam replied.

"Then why did you?" asked the Father.

"I don't know," said Eve.

"She started it!" Adam said.

"Did not!"

"Did too!"

"DID NOT!"

Having had it with the two of them,
    God's punishment was that Adam
    and Eve should have children of their own.
    Thus, the pattern was set and it has never changed.

Things I've Learned From My Children

1. A king-size waterbed holds enough water to fill a 2000 square foot ranch house 1/4-inch deep.

2. If you spray hair spray on dust bunnies and run over them with Roller Blades, they can ignite.

3. A 3-year-old's voice is louder than 200 adults in a crowded restaurant.

4. If you hook a dog leash over a ceiling fan, the motor is not strong enough to rotate a 42-pound boy wearing Batman underwear and a Superman cape. It is strong enough, however, if tied to a paint can, to spread paint on all four walls of a 20-by-20 foot room.

5. You should not throw baseballs up when the ceiling fan is on. When using the ceiling fan as a bat, you have to throw the ball up a few times before you get a hit. A ceiling fan can hit a baseball a long way.

6. The glass in windows (even double pane) doesn't stop a baseball hit by a ceiling fan.

7. When you hear the toilet flush and the words "Uh-oh," it's already too late.

8. Brake fluid mixed with Clorox bleach makes smoke— and lots of it.

9. Certain LEGOs will pass through the digestive tract of a 4-year-old.

10. "Play Dough" and "microwave" should never be used in the same sentence.

11. No matter how much Jell-O you put in a swimming pool, you still can't walk on water.

Words of Wisdom From Children

Never allow your 3-year-old brother in the same room as your school assignment.
> **–Traci, age 14**

Don't pick on your sister when she's holding a baseball bat.
> **–Joel, age 10**

When your dad is mad and asks you, "Do I look stupid?" don't answer him.
> **–Michael, age 14**

Never tell your mom her diet's not working.
> **–Michael, age 14**

Stay away from prunes.
> **–Randy, age 9**

Never try to baptize a cat.
> **–Eileen, age 8**

Never trust a dog to watch your food.
> **–Patrick, age 10**

Puppies still have bad breath, even after eating a Tic Tac.
> **–Andrew, age 9**

Never hold a Dust Buster and a cat at the same time.
> **–Kyoyo, age 9**

If you want a kitten, start out by asking for a horse.
> **–Naomi, age 15**

Honesty

A toddler came screaming out of the bathroom to tell his mom he'd dropped his toothbrush in the toilet. She fished it out and threw it in the garbage. The toddler stood there thinking for a moment, then ran to his mom's bathroom and came out with her toothbrush. He held it up and said with a charming little smile, "We better throw this one out too then, 'cause it fell in the toilet a few days ago."

Who's Home?

A salesman telephoned a household, and a 4–year-old boy answered. The conversation went like this . . .

Salesman: May I speak to your mother?
Boy: She's not here.
Salesman: Well, is anyone else there?
Boy: My sister.
Salesman: OK, fine. May I speak to her?
Boy: I guess so.

At this point there was a very long silence on the phone. Then . . .

Boy: Hello?
Salesman: It's you. I thought you were going to to call your sister?
Boy: I did. The trouble is, I can't get her out of the playpen.

Nudity

A mother was driving with her three young children one warm summer evening when a woman in the convertible ahead of them stood up and waved. She was stark naked! Reeling from the shock, the mother heard her 5-year-old shout from the back seat, "Mom! That lady isn't wearing a seat belt!"

More Nudity

A little boy got lost at the YMCA and found himself in the women's locker room. When he was spotted, the women in the room burst into shrieks, with ladies grabbing towels and running for cover. The little boy watched in amazement and then asked, "What's the matter, haven't you ever seen a little boy before?"

Smarter Than You Think

A teenage boy with spiked hair, nose ring, and baggy clothes was overheard telling a friend, "I don't really like to dress like this, but it keeps my parents from dragging me everywhere with them."

Opinions

On the first day of school, a first-grader handed his teacher a note from his mother. The note read, "The opinions expressed by this child are not necessarily those of his parents."

Dress Up

A little girl was watching her parents dress for a party. When she saw her dad donning his tuxedo, she warned, "Daddy, you shouldn't wear that suit."

"Why not, darling?"

"You know it always gives you a headache the next morning."

Ketchup

A woman was trying hard to get the ketchup to come out of the container. During her struggle the phone rang, so she asked her 4-year-old daughter to answer it. "It's the minister, Mommy," the child said. Then she told the caller, "Mommy can't come to the phone to talk to you right now. She's hitting the bottle."

Accelerated Conversation

A 4-year-old was eating an apple in the back seat of the car, when he asked, "Daddy, why is my apple turning brown?"

"Because," his dad explained, "after you ate the skin off, the meat of the apple came into contact with the air, which caused it to oxidize, thus changing the molecular structure and turning it into a different color."

There was a long silence. Then the boy asked, "Daddy, are you talking to me?"

A Proper Burial

While walking along the sidewalk in front of his church, a minister heard the intoning of a prayer that nearly made his collar wilt. Apparently his 5-year-old son and his playmates had found a dead bird. Feeling that proper burial should be performed, they had secured a small box and cotton batting, then dug a hole and made ready for the disposal of the deceased. The minister's son was chosen to say the appropriate prayers, and with sonorous dignity the boy intoned his version of what he thought his father always said: "Glory be unto the Faaaather, and unto the Sonn . . . and into the hole he gooooes."

Police

While taking a routine
vandalism report at
an elementary school,
a policeman was interrupted by
a little girl about 6 years old. Looking up and down at
his uniform, she asked, "Are you a cop?"

"Yes," he answered and continued writing the report.

"My mother said if I ever needed help, I should ask the
police. Is that right?"

"Yes, that's right," he told her.

"Well, then," she said as she extended her foot toward him,
"would you please tie my shoe?"

More Police

It was the end of the day when a police officer parked his van
in front of the station. As he gathered his equipment, his
K-9 partner was barking, and he saw a little boy staring in
at him. "Is that a dog you got back there?" he asked.

"It sure is," the policeman replied.

Puzzled, the boy looked at him and then toward the back
of the van. Finally, he said, "What'd he do?"

Cute Words

"Close the curtains," requested a 2-year-old sitting in a pool of bright light. "The sun's looking at me too hard."

. . .

When asked when he would turn 6, a young boy replied, "When I'm tired of being 5."

. . .

Seeing her first hailstorm, a toddler exclaimed, "Mommy, it's raining dumplings!"

. . .

While a mom frantically waved away a pesky fly with a white dish towel, her daughter observed, "Maybe he thinks you're surrendering."

. . .

A grandfather was reading to his 4-year-old grandson about Adam and Eve. The boy asked, "Is this where God took out the man's brain and made a woman?"

. . .

Mom told daughter Lori that the little girl's aunt just had a baby and that it looked like her uncle. "You mean he has a mustache?" Lori asked.

. . .

When asked if he could name the capital of Florida, a child fired right back, "Capital F!"

. . .

While shampooing a son's hair, a mom noted his hair was growing so fast he'd soon need to get it cut. He replied, "Maybe we shouldn't water it so much."

A mother told her young daughter that their SUV was going to be fixed. Instantly, the small fry said, "Oh, it's going to the tire-o-practor?"

. . .

Impressed by the 5-year-old's vocabulary, a neighbor complimented the young scholar, who nonchalantly responded, "I have words in my head I haven't even used yet."

. . .

When Tommy asked about two look-alike classmates at school, his mom told him they were probably twins. The next day, he came home from school all bubbly and said, "Guess what? Not only are they twins . . . they're brothers!"

. . .

Mom informed her son, Brian, that she was going outside to get a little sun. "But Mommy," he gulped, "you already have a son. Me!"

Beauty Secrets

Little Johnny watched, fascinated, as his mother smoothed cold cream on her face.

"Why do you do that, Mommy?" he asked.

"To make myself beautiful," said his mother, who then began removing the cream with a tissue.

"What's the matter?" asked Little Johnny. "Giving up?"

Elderly

A 4-year-old accompanied her mother as she delivered lunches to elderly shut-ins. She was unfailingly intrigued by the various appliances of old age, particularly the canes, walkers, and wheelchairs. One day the mother found her staring at a pair of false teeth soaking in a glass. As she braced herself for the inevitable barrage of questions, she merely turned and whispered, "The tooth fairy will never believe this!"

Special Coffee

A grandmother was surprised
by her 7-year-old grandson
one morning. He had made her
coffee. She drank what was the worst cup of coffee
in her life. When she got to the bottom, she found
three of those little green army men. She said, "Honey,
what are the army men doing in my coffee?"

Her grandson said, "Grandma, it says on TV 'The best part
of waking up is soldiers in your cup!'"

A Young Author

A 3-year-old was diligently pounding away at her father's
word processor.

Her dad asked her what she was doing.

"Writing a story," she answered.

"What's it about?" he asked.

"I don't know," she replied. "I can't read."

Animal Sounds

A group of young children were in the backyard playing school. One child was playing "teacher" and asking them all questions.

"Davy, what noise does a cow make?"

"It goes moo."

"Alice, what noise does a cat make?"

"It goes meow."

"Jamie, what sound does a lamb make?"

"It goes baaa."

"Jennifer, what sound does a mouse make?"

"Errr . . . it goes . . . click!"

Who's in Charge?

One evening a preschooler, Krystal, and her parents were sitting on the couch chatting. Krystal asked, "Daddy, you're the boss of the house, right?"

Her father proudly replied, "Yes, I am the boss of the house."

But Krystal quickly burst his bubble when she added "Cause Mommy put you in charge, huh Daddy?"

Career Exploration

On the way to preschool, a doctor had left her stethoscope on the car seat, and her little girl picked it up and began playing with it.

"Be still, my heart," thought the doctor, "my daughter wants to follow in my footsteps!"

Then the child spoke into the instrument: "Welcome to McDonald's. May I take your order?"

Rules According to a Child

If I like it, it's mine.

If it's in my hand, it's mine.

If I can take it from you, it's mine.

If I had it a little while ago, it's mine.

If it's mine, it must never appear to be yours in any way.

If I'm doing or building something, all the pieces are mine.

If it looks just like mine, it is mine.

If I think it's mine, it's mine.

If I saw it first, it's mine.

If you are playing with something and you put it down, it automatically becomes mine.

If it's broken, it's yours!

Girl and Her Grandpa

A little girl got on her grandpa's lap and asked, "Did God make me?"

"Yes," he said.

"Did God make you, too?"

"Yes," the grandpa replied.

"Well," the little girl said, while running her fingers down his wrinkles and looking at his thinning hair, "he sure is doing a better job nowadays."

Kids' Verses

"God bless America, through the night with a light from a bulb!"

. . .

"O Susanna, O don't you cry for me, for I come from Alabama with a band-aid on my knee!"

. . .

"Give us this day our deli bread! Glory be to the Father, and to the Son, and to the whole East Coast."

. . .

"We shall come to Joyce's, bringing in the cheese."

. . .

"Yield not to Penn Station, but deliver us from evil."

The Fat of It

Realizing that she'd put on a pound or two, a wife lamented to her husband, "I'm fat."

Right on cue he said what all good husbands must: "No you're not!" To support his position, he added, "Just take a look at some of the other women we know, and you'll see that you are not fat."

Their daughter, a high schooler, saw through it and said: "Mom, he's grading you on the curve!"

White Hair

One day, a little girl was sitting and watching her mother do the dishes at the kitchen sink. She suddenly noticed several strands of white hair sticking out in contrast to her mother's brunette head.

The girl asked, "Why are some of your hairs white, Mom?"

Her mother answered, "Well, every time you do something wrong and make me cry or make me unhappy, one of my hairs turns white."

The little girl thought this revelation over for a while, then asked, "Mom, why are ALL of grandma's hairs white?"

Hamburger Seeds

A dad took his 4-year-old son to McDonald's for dinner one evening for a "guys night out."

As they were eating their hamburgers, the son asked, "Daddy, what are these little things on the hamburger buns?"

The dad explained that they were tiny seeds and that they were OK to eat.

The boy was quiet for a couple of minutes obviously in deep thought.

Finally, the youth looked up and said, "Daddy, if we go home and plant these seeds in our backyard, we will have enough hamburgers to last forever."

The New Reader

A family took their first-grader on a car trip to Canada. To help pass the time, the boy practiced his new reading skills by calling out road signs.

Then he fell asleep just before they entered Quebec.

When he woke up he saw the French highway signs and said in a worried tone, "I think I forgot how to read while I was asleep."

Sissy!

One summer evening during a violent thunderstorm, a mother was tucking her son into bed. She was about to turn off the light when he asked with a trembling voice, "Mommy, will you sleep with me tonight?"

The mother smiled and gave him a reassuring hug. "I can't dear," she said, "I have to sleep in Daddy's room."

A long silence was broken at last by his shaky little voice, saying, "The big sissy."

Dead or Alive

A kindergarten pupil told his teacher he'd found a cat. She asked him if it was dead or alive. "Dead," he told her.

"How do you know?" she asked.

"Because I pissed in its ear, and it didn't move," answered the child innocently.

"You did what?!" the teacher exclaimed in surprise.

"You know," explained the boy, "I leaned over and went 'Pssst!' and it didn't move."

What's Growing?

A pregnant mother's 3-year-old came into the room when she was just getting ready to get into the shower. She said, "Mommy, you are getting fat!"

She replied, "Yes, honey. Remember, Mommy has a baby growing in her tummy."

"I know," the child replied, "but what's growing in your butt?"

In and Out of Heaven

An exasperated mother, whose son was always getting into mischief, finally asked him, "How do you expect to get into Heaven?"

The boy thought it over and said, "Well, I'll run in and out and in and out and keep slamming the door until St. Peter says, 'For Heaven's sake, Dylan, come in or stay out!'"

Sack Races

At a school picnic, a son asked his mother if she'd take part in the mother-son relay games with him. She told him she would and to let her know when they were to begin.

As soon as the gunnysack race was announced, Timmy came bounding across the field and shouted:

"Mommy, hurry! It's time for the old-bag race, and we're all waiting for you."

They Grow Up So Fast!

A 2-year-old walked into the bathroom while her mother was putting on makeup.

"I'm going to look just like you, Mommy!" announced the little girl.

"Maybe, when you grow up," her mother told her.

"No, Mommy, tomorrow," asserted the little girl. "I just put on that 'Oil of Old Lady' you always use."

Ironing

During the Sunday morning service, it was time for the children's sermon. All the children were invited to come forward. One little girl was wearing a particularly pretty dress and, as she sat down, the pastor leaned over and said, "That is a very pretty dress. Is it your Easter dress?"

The little girl replied directly into the pastor's clip-on microphone, "Yes, and my mom says it's a bitch to iron."

A Drink of Water

A small boy is sent to bed by his father. Five minutes later, ". . . Da-ad . . ."

"What?"

"I'm thirsty. Can you bring me a drink of water?"

"No. You had your chance. Lights out."

Five minutes later, "Da-aaaad . . ."

"What?"

"I'm thirsty. Can I have a drink of water??"

"I told you NO! If you ask again, I'll have to spank you!!"

Five minutes later, "Daaaa-aaaad . . ."

"What?"

"When you come in to spank me, can you bring a drink of water?"

The New Math

A little boy was doing his math homework. He said to himself, "Two plus five, that son of a bitch is seven. Three plus six, that son of a bitch is nine . . ."

His mother heard what he was saying and gasped, "What are you doing?"

The little boy answered, "I'm doing my math homework, Mom."

"And this is how your teacher taught you to do it?" the mother asked.

"Yes," he answered.

Infuriated, the mother asked the teacher the next day, "What are you teaching my son in math?"

The teacher replied, "Right now, we are learning addition."

The mother asked, "And are you teaching them to say 'Two plus two, that son of a bitch is four?'"

After the teacher stopped laughing, she answered, "What I taught them was, two plus two, THE SUM OF WHICH is four."

23

Darn Kids

A salesman calls this house, and the 3-year-old son
  answers the phone.

The salesman asks, "Can I talk to your mother?"

The boy whispers in a very low voice, "She's busy."

The salesman asks, "Can I talk to your daddy?"

The kid whispers again, in a very low voice, "He's busy too."

The salesman then asks, "Is there anyone else there?"

The tot replies in the same quiet voice, "A policeman."

The salesman inquires, "Can I talk to the policeman?"

The boy repeats again, in a low whisper, "He's busy too."

The salesman again questions him and asks, "Is there
  anyone else there?"

The kid comes back in a whisper, "A fireman."

The salesman then wants to know
  if he can talk to the fireman.
  And once again the tot
  whispers, "He's busy too."

By now the salesman is really
  wondering what is going on.

He asks the boy, "What are they
  all doing?"

The little rug-rat replies, still
  in a very low whisper . . .

"Looking for me."

Perfect Cupcakes

A young boy was helping ice the cupcakes for his father's birthday.

"The cupcakes look delicious, Tim." his dad said. He took a bite while looking at the other cupcakes.

"Tim, these are so good."

As he finished one and took another he again complimented his son. "The cupcakes look beautiful, Tim. How did you get them iced so evenly?" And he took a large bite while waiting for the answer.

His son replied, "I licked them."

Where Did I Come From?

"Daddy, where did I come from?" the 7-year-old asked.

It was a moment for which her parents had carefully prepared. They took her into the living room, got out the encyclopedia and several other books, and explained all they thought she should know about sexual attraction, affection, love, and reproduction. Then they both sat back and smiled contentedly.

"Does that answer your question?" her father asked.

"Not really," the little girl said. "Marcia said she came from Detroit. I want to know where I came from."

Thoughts on Love

What is the proper age to get married?

Once I'm done with kindergarten, I'm going to find a wife.

　　–Tom, 5

What do most people do on a date?

On the first date, they just tell each other lies, and that usually gets them interested enough to go for a second date.

　　–Mike, 9

When is it OK to kiss someone?

You should never kiss a girl unless you have enough bucks to buy her a big ring and her own VCR, 'cause she'll want to have videos of the wedding.

　　–Jim, 10

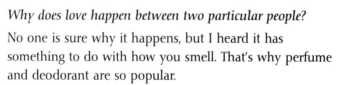

Why does love happen between two particular people?

No one is sure why it happens, but I heard it has something to do with how you smell. That's why perfume and deodorant are so popular.

　　–Jan, 9

What is falling in love like?

Like an avalanche where you have to run for your life.

　　–Roger, 9

How long does it take to fall in love?

If falling in love is anything like learning how to spell, I don't want to do it. It takes too long.

　　–Leo, 7

Are good looks important in love?

If you want to be loved by somebody who isn't already in your family, it doesn't hurt to be beautiful.

–Jeanne, 8

It isn't always how you look. Look at me, I'm handsome like anything and I haven't got anybody to marry me yet.

–Gary, 7

Is beauty or money more important in love?

Beauty is only skin deep. But how rich you are can last a long time.

–Christine, 9

Wedding Vows

A grandmother overheard her 5-year-old granddaughter playing "wedding."

The wedding vows went like this:

"You have the right to remain silent. Anything you say may be held against you. You have the right to have an attorney present. You may kiss the bride."

What Does Love Mean?

A group of professional psychologists posed this question to a group of 4- through 8-year-olds: "What does love mean?"

Love is that first feeling you feel before all the bad stuff gets in the way.

Love is when a girl puts on perfume and a boy puts on shaving cologne and they go out and smell each other.

Love is when you go out to eat and give somebody most of your french fries without making them give you any of theirs.

Love is like a little old woman and a little old man who are still friends even after they know each other so well.

Love is when my mommy makes coffee for my daddy and she takes a sip before giving it to him to make sure the taste is OK.

Love is when your puppy licks your face even after you left him alone all day.

Love is when Mommy gives Daddy the best piece of chicken.

Love is when Mommy sees Daddy smelly and sweaty and still says he is handsomer than Robert Redford.

I know my older sister loves me because she gives me all her old clothes and has to go out and buy new ones.

Love is what's in the room with you at Christmas if you stop opening presents and listen.

Love cards like Valentine's cards say stuff on them that we'd like to say ourselves, but we wouldn't be caught dead saying.

teaching

Actual Rules for Teachers
(circa 1915)

1. You will not marry during the term of your contract.

2. You are not to keep company with men.

3. You must be home between the hours of 8 P.M. and 6 A.M. unless attending a school function.

4. Your dresses must not be any shorter than two inches above the ankle.

5. You may not travel beyond the city limits unless you have the permission of the chairman of the school board.

6. You may not ride in a carriage or automobile with any man unless he is your father or brother.

7. You may not dress in bright colors.

8. You may under no circumstances dye your hair.

9. You must wear at least two petticoats.

10. You may not loiter downtown in ice cream stores.

Are You Acting Too Much Like a Teacher?

1. Do you ask guests if they have remembered their scarves and mittens as they leave your home?

2. Do you move your dinner partner's glass away from the edge of the table?

3. Do you ask if anyone needs to go to the bathroom as you enter a theater with a group of friends?

4. Do you hand a tissue to anyone who sneezes?

5. Do you refer to happy hour as "snack time"?

6. Do you declare "no cuts" when a shopper squeezes ahead of you in a checkout line?

7. Do you say, "I like the way you did that" to the mechanic who repairs your car nicely?

8. Do you ask, "Are you sure you did your best?" to the mechanic who fails to repair your car to your satisfaction?

9. Do you sing "The Alphabet Song" to yourself as you look up a number in the phone book?

10. Do you say everything twice? I mean, do you repeat everything?

11. Do you fold your spouse's fingers over the coins as you hand him/her money at a tollbooth?

12. Do you ask a quiet person at a party if he has something to share with the group?

The Challenges of Teaching

After being interviewed by the school administration,
the eager teaching prospect said: Let me see if I've got
this right—

You want me to go into that room with all those kids and
fill their every waking moment with a love for learning.

I'm supposed to instill a sense of pride in their ethnicity,
modify their disruptive behavior, observe them for signs
of abuse, and even censor their T-shirt messages and
dress habits.

You want me to teach them patriotism, good citizenship,
sportsmanship and fair play, how and where to register
to vote, how to balance a checkbook, and how to apply
for a job.

I am to check their heads for lice, maintain a safe environment, recognize signs of antisocial behavior, offer
advice, write letters of recommendation for student
employment and scholarships, encourage respect for the
cultural diversity of others, and, oh yes, always make
sure that I give the girls in my class at least 50 percent
of my attention.

My contract requires me to work on my own time after
school and evenings grading papers. Also, I must
spend my summer vacation working toward advanced
certification and a master's degree, at my own expense,
of course.

And on my own time you want me to attend committee
and faculty meetings, PTA meetings, and participate
in staff development training.

I am to be a paragon of virtue, larger than life, such that my very presence will awe my students into being obedient and respectful of authority. In addition, I am to pledge allegiance to family values and the politically correct whims of the teachers' unions, no matter how paradoxical those two ideas may be!

You want me to incorporate technology into the learning experience, monitor Web sites, and relate personally with each student. That includes deciding who might be potentially dangerous and/or liable to commit a crime at school.

I am to make sure all students, even those who don't come to school regularly or complete any of their assignments, pass the mandatory exams.
Plus, I am to make sure that all of the students with handicaps get an equal education regardless of the extent of their mental or physical disability.

And I am to communicate regularly with parents by letter, telephone, newsletter, and report card.

All of this I am to do with just one piece of chalk; a shared, outdated computer; a few books; the district-mandated regulation bulletin bored (er, board); and a big smile on a starting salary that qualifies my family for food stamps!

You want me to do all of this, and you expect me . . .

NOT TO PRAY ? !

The Next Survivor

Three businessmen and three business-women will be dropped in an elementary school classroom for 6 weeks. Each businessperson will be provided with a copy of the school district's curriculum and have a class of 28 students to teach.

Each class will have five learning disabled children, three with ADD, one gifted child, and two who have limited English proficiency. And three will be identified as having severe behavior problems.

Each businessperson must complete lesson plans at least 3 days in advance, with annotations for curriculum objectives, and modify, organize, or create materials accordingly. He or she will be required to teach students, handle misconduct, implement technology, document attendance, write referrals, correct home-work, make bulletin boards, compute grades, complete report cards, document benchmarks, communicate with parents, and arrange parent conferences.

They must also supervise recess and monitor the hallways. In addition, they will complete drills for fire, tornadoes, or shooting attacks. They must attend workshops, faculty meetings, union meetings, and curriculum development meetings. They must also tutor those students who are behind and strive to get their non–English–speaking students proficient enough to take the state assessment exams.

If the businesspeople are sick or having a bad day, they must not let it show. Each day they must incorporate reading, writing, math, science, and social studies into the program. They must maintain discipline and provide an educationally stimulating environment at all times.

They will have access to the golf course only on the weekends, but on their new salary they will not be able to afford golf anyway. There will be no access to vendors who want to take them to lunch—and lunch will be limited to 30 minutes, 10 of which must be spent walking students to the cafeteria, getting them through the lunch lines, and seating them at the correct table.

On days when they do not have recess duty, the businesspeople will be permitted to use the staff restroom—as long as another survival candidate is supervising their class.

They will be provided with two 40-minute planning periods per week while their students are at "specials." If the copier is operable, they may make copies of necessary materials at this time.

The businesspeople must continually advance their education on their own time and pay for this advanced training themselves. This can be accomplished by moonlighting at a second job or marrying someone with money. The winner will be allowed to return to his/her job in the business world.

School Answering Service

You have reached the automated answering service of your school. In order to assist you in connecting to the right staff member, please listen to all options before making a selection:

To lie about why your child is absent
   —Press 1

To make excuses for why your child did not do his work
   —Press 2

To complain about what we do
   —Press 3

To cuss out staff members
   —Press 4

To ask why you didn't get needed information that was already enclosed in your newsletter and several bulletins mailed to you
   —Press 5

To request another teacher for the third time this year
   —Press 6

If you want to reach out and touch, slap, or hit someone
   —Press 7

If you want us to raise you child
   —Press 8

To complain about bus transportation
   —Press 9

To complain about school lunches
    —Press 0

If you realize this is the real world and your child must be accountable/responsible for his/her own behavior, classwork, homework, and that your child's lack of effort is NOT the teacher's fault . . .

—HANG UP and HAVE A NICE DAY!!!

You Might Be a Teacher If . . .

You want to slap the next person who says, "Must be nice to have all of your holidays and summers free."

You can tell it's a full moon without ever looking outside.

You believe "shallow gene pool" should have its own box on the report card.

When out in public, you feel the urge to talk to strange children and correct their behavior.

You think people should be required to get a government permit before being allowed to reproduce.

You can't have children of your own because there is NO name you could ever give a child that wouldn't bring on high blood pressure the moment you heard it.

Meeting a child's parent INSTANTLY answers the question, "Why is this kid like this?"

Texas Teacher

Did you hear about the Texas
teacher who was helping one
of her kindergarten students
put on his cowboy boots?

He asked for help, and she could see why. Even with her
pulling and him pushing, the little boots still didn't
want to go on.

By the time the second boot was on, she had worked
up a sweat.

She almost cried when the little boy said, "Teacher, they're
on the wrong feet." She looked and sure enough, they
were.

It wasn't any easier pulling the boots off than it was
putting them on. She managed to keep her cool as
together they worked to get the boots on the right feet.

He then announced, "These aren't my boots."

She bit her tongue rather than get in his face and scream,
"Why didn't you say so?" like she wanted to.

And, once again she struggled to help him pull the ill-
fitting boots off his little feet.

They got the boots off and he immediately said, "They're
my brother's boots. My mom made me wear 'em."

Now she didn't know if she should laugh or cry. But
she mustered up the grace and courage she had left
to wrestle the boots on his feet again.

Helping him into his coat, she asked, "Now, where are
your mittens?"

He said, "I stuffed 'em in the toes of my boots."

Who's There?

Three people were trying to get into Heaven.

St. Peter asked the first, "Who's there?"

"It's me, Albert Jones," a voice replied.

St. Peter let him in.

St. Peter asked the second one the same question, "Who's there?"

"It's me, Charlie Smith."

St. Peter let him in, too.

He finally asked the third one, "Who's there?"

"It is I, Verla Mara," answered the third.

"Oh, great," muttered St. Peter. "Another one of those English teachers."

Fair Is Fair!

Little Johnny had finished his summer vacation and gone back to school. Two days later his teacher phoned his mother to tell her that he was misbehaving.

"Wait a minute," the mother said. "I had Johnny with me for two months, and I never called you once when he misbehaved!"

A Proper Sentence?

The teacher wrote "Like I ain't had no fun in months" on the blackboard.

Then she said, "Tommy, how should I correct that?"

Tommy replied, "Get a new boyfriend?"

An Obvious Answer

During an English lesson, the teacher asked her students, "Now tell me, what do you call a person who keeps on talking when people are no longer interested?"

Little Susie, in the back row, replied, "A teacher!"

Homework Instructions

According to the Official Handbook of Proper Parenting, students should not spend more than 90 minutes working on their homework assignments. . . . These 90 minutes should be budgeted in the following manner:

15 minutes looking for assignment.

11 minutes calling a friend for the assignment.

23 minutes explaining why the teacher is mean and just does not like children.

6 minutes telling parents that the teacher never explained the assignment.

7 minutes checking the *TV Guide*.

8 minutes in the bathroom.

10 minutes getting a snack.

10 minutes sitting at the kitchen table waiting for Mom or Dad to do the assignment.

Teachers' Pay

Teachers are paid too much! I'm fed up with teachers and their hefty salaries for only 9 months' work! What we need here is a little perspective. If I had my way, I'd pay teachers babysitting wages.

That's right. Instead of paying these outrageous taxes, I'd give them $3.00 an hour. And I'm only going to pay them for 5 hours, not planning time. That would be $15.00 a day. Each parent should pay $15.00 a day for these teachers to babysit their children. Even if they have more than one child, it's still cheaper than private day care.

Now how many children do they teach a day— maybe 20? That's $15.00 x 20 = $300.00 a day. But remember, they only work 180 days a year! I'm not going to pay them for all the vacations: $300.00 x 180 = $54,000.

Just a minute, my calculator must need batteries.

What will teachers say about those who have 10 years of experience and a Master's degree? Well, maybe (just to be fair) they could get the minimum wage. We can round that off to about $6.00 an hour, times 5 hours, times 20 children. $6.00 x 5 x 20. That's $600 a day times 180 days. That's only $108,000.

Wait a minute! There is something wrong here.

school daze

First Day of School

A child came home from his first day at school.
His mother asked, "Well, what did you learn today?"
The kid replied, "Not enough. They
    want me to come back tomorrow."

First Week of School

A little girl had just finished her first week of school. "I'm
    just wasting my time," she said to her mother. "I can't
    read, I can't write, and they won't let me talk!"

School Days

Tommy had reached school age. His mother managed with
    a blast of propaganda to make him enthusiastic about
    the idea. She bought him lots of new clothes, told him
    of the new friends he'd meet, and so on.

The first day came. He eagerly went off and came back
    home with a lot of glowing reports about school.

The next morning when his mom woke him up early
    again, he asked, "What for?"

She told him it was time to get ready for school.

"What, again?" he asked.

Kindergarten Gifts

It was the end of the school year and a kindergarten teacher was receiving gifts from her pupils.

The florist's son handed her a gift. She shook it, held it overhead, and said, "I bet I know what this is. Is it flowers?"

"That's right," the boy said, "but how did you know?"

"Oh, just a wild guess," she replied.

The next pupil was the daughter of the sweet shop owner. The teacher held her gift overhead, shook it, and said, "I bet I know what this is. Is it a box of sweets?"

"That's right, but how did you know?" asked the girl.

"Oh, just another wild guess," said the teacher.

The next gift was from the son of the liquor store owner. The teacher held the gift overhead and noticed that it was leaking. She touched a drop of the liquid with her finger and then touched it to her tongue.

"Is it wine?" she asked.

"No," the boy replied with some excitement.

The teacher repeated the process, taking a larger drop of the leakage to her tongue.

"Is it champagne?" she asked.

"No," the boy replied with more excitement.

The teacher took one more taste before declaring, "I give up. What is it?"

With great glee the boy replied, "It's a puppy!"

Two Fingers

On the first day of school, the kindergarten teacher instructed,

"If anyone has to go to the bathroom, hold up two fingers."

A little voice from the back of the class asked,

"How will that help?"

Pledge of Allegiance

Johnny was at his first day of school.

The teacher advised the class that they would start the day with the Pledge of Allegiance, and instructed them to put their right hands over their hearts and repeat after her.

As she started the recitation, she looked around the room. "I pledge allegiance to the flag...." When her eyes fell on Johnny, she found that he had his hand over the right cheek of his buttocks.

"Johnny, I will not continue until you put your hand over your heart," the teacher said.

Johnny replied, "It is over my heart."

After several failed attempts to correct Johnny's posture, the teacher finally asked him, "Why do you think that is your heart?"

"Because," answered Johnny, "every time my grandma comes to visit, she picks me up and pats me here and says, 'Bless your little heart!' And my grandma wouldn't lie!"

What Does God Look Like?

A kindergarten teacher was observing her students while they drew. She would occasionally walk around the classroom to see each child's artwork. As she came to one little girl who was working diligently, she asked what the drawing was.

The girl replied, "I'm drawing God."

The teacher paused and said, "But no one knows what God looks like."

Without missing a beat or looking up from her drawing, the girl replied, "They will in a minute."

Good Luck Dogs

A nursery school teacher was delivering a minivan full of kids home one day when a fire truck zoomed past. Sitting in the front seat of the fire truck was a Dalmatian dog. The children started discussing the dog's duties.

"They use him to keep crowds back," said one youngster.

"No," said another, "he's just for good luck."

A third child brought the argument to a close. "They use the dog," she said firmly, "to find the fire hydrant."

Music Notes

The first-graders were attending their first music lesson.

The teacher began the lesson with some fundamentals. She drew a musical staff on the board and asked a little girl to come up to write a note on it.

The little girl went to the board, looked thoughtfully for a minute and wrote:

"Dear Aunt Emma, just a short note to tell you I'm fine."

Navigating in School

Little Jimmy, in his first day at a new school, raised his hand for "number one" and asked how to find the boy's room.

After getting directions, he left the classroom. He returned a few minutes later and said to the teacher, "I couldn't find it."

The teacher asked Bobby, who was familiar with the school, to show Jimmy the way.

When they returned, the teacher asked Bobby why he thought Jimmy had trouble finding it, since it was right around the corner from the classroom.

Bobby replied, "He had his shorts on backwards."

Expecting

For weeks, a 6-year-old lad had been telling his first-grade teacher about the baby brother or sister that was expected at his house.

Then one day, the boy's mother allowed him to feel the movements of the unborn child. The 6-year-old was obviously impressed but made no comment. Furthermore, he stopped telling his teacher about the impending event.

The concerned teacher finally sat the boy on her lap and asked, "Tommy, whatever has become of that baby brother or sister you were expecting at home?"

Tommy burst into tears and confessed, "I think Mommy ate it!"

Public Servant

"Give me a sentence about a public servant," said a teacher.

The small boy wrote, "The fireman came down the ladder pregnant."

The teacher took the lad aside to correct him. "Don't you know what pregnant means?" she asked.

"Sure," said the young boy confidently. "It means carrying a child."

Proverbs?

A first-grade teacher collected well-known proverbs. She gave each child in her class the first half of a proverb and asked them to come up with the remainder of the proverb. It's hard to believe these were actually done by first-graders, but there are some good ones nonetheless. Their insights may surprise you.

Better to be safe than...

punch a fifth grader.

Strike while the...

bug is close.

It's always darkest before...

daylight savings time.

Never underestimate the power of...

termites.

You can lead a horse to water but...

how?

Don't bite the hand that...

looks dirty.

No news is...

impossible.

A miss is as good as a...

Mr.

You can't teach an old dog new...

math.

If you lie down with dogs, you'll...

stink in the morning.

Love all, trust...

me.

The pen is mightier than the...

pigs.

Where there's smoke, there's...

pollution.

Happy is the bride who...

gets all the presents.

A penny saved is...

not much.

Two's company, three's...

the Musketeers.

Don't put off till tomorrow what...

you put on to go to bed.

Laugh and the whole world laughs with you, cry and...

you have to blow your nose.

Children should be seen and not...

spanked or grounded.

If at first you don't succeed...

get new batteries.

You get out of something only what you...

see in the picture on the box.

When the blind leadeth the blind...

get out of the way.

Better late than...

pregnant.

Discovering America

Teacher: George, go to the map and find North America.

Student: Here it is!

Teacher: Correct. Now class, who discovered America?

Class: George!!

Who Are You?

Substitute Teacher: Are you chewing gum?

Student: No, I'm Billy Anderson.

Promises! Promises!

Teacher: Didn't you promise to behave?

Student: Yes, Sir.

Teacher: And didn't I promise to punish you if you didn't?

Student: Yes, Sir, but since I broke my promise, I don't expect you to keep yours.

Hopes

Teacher: I hope I didn't see you looking at Don's paper.

John: I hope you didn't either.

Punishment

Harold: Teacher, would you punish me for something I didn't do?

Teacher: Of course not.

Harold: Good, because I didn't do my homework.

Late Excuse

Teacher: Why are you late?

Student: Because of the sign.

Teacher: What sign?

Student: The one that says, "School Ahead, Slow Children Crossing."

Science Lesson

Mr. Smythe had been giving his second–grade students a lesson on science. He had explained about magnets, and showed how they would pick up nails and other bits of iron.

And now it was question time. "Class," asked Mr. Smythe, "my name begins with the letter 'M' and I pick up things. What am I?"

A little boy in the front row answered, "You're a mother!"

A Barrel of Laughs

A teacher asked her students if they could use the words "defeat," "defense," and "detail" in a sentence.

Little Joey, the smart alec, answered, "De feet of de dog went over de fence before de tail."

Complicated Arithmetic

The math teacher saw that Billy wasn't paying attention in class. She called on him and said, "Billy? What are 2 and 4 and 28 and 44?"

He quickly replied, "NBC, CBS, HBO, and the Cartoon Network!"

Aptitude Test

Little Johnny wanted to be an accountant, so he took an aptitude test and this is how it went:

Mr. Proctor: If I give you two rabbits, and two rabbits, and another two rabbits, how many rabbits do you have?

Little Johnny: SEVEN!

Mr. Proctor: No, listen again carefully. If I give you two rabbits, and two rabbits, and another two rabbits, how many rabbits do you have?

Little Johnny: SEVEN!

Mr. Proctor: Let's try this another way. If I give you two bottles of pop, and two bottles of pop, and another two bottles of pop, how many bottles of pop do you have?

Little Johnny: SIX.

Mr. Proctor: Good! Now, if I give you two rabbits, and two rabbits, and another two rabbits, how many rabbits do you have?

Little Johnny: SEVEN!

Mr. Proctor: How on earth do you work out that three lots of two rabbits are seven?

Little Johnny: I already have one rabbit at home!

Dear Third-Grade Diary

Hi, I'm in third grade, but it's not easy; it's a jungle gym out there.

It's not school I mind—it's the principal of the thing.

My teacher is tough. In class we have to answer "Yes, Sir" and "No, Sir," and my teacher is a woman.

She's cross-eyed too; can't control her pupils.

In English she told us we couldn't use two words, one was cool and the other was lousy. I said, "Cool, tell us the lousy one first."

In science, she asked, "What would happen if one of the stars in Orion's belt went out?" I told her that his pants would fall down.

She asked, "Why do astronauts wear space suits?" I said, "To cover their space underwear."

In geography she asked us to name two cities in Kentucky. I said "OK, I'll name one Waldo and the other Heathcliff."

And I don't like math at all; there are just too many problems.

We eat in the cafeteria. For lunch yesterday we had roast beef, bread, and butter. The roast beef was so tough it challenged me to a fight after school. The bread was so stale I took it to show and tell in history class. I'd tell you about the butter, but I don't want to spread it around.

They gave us animal crackers for dessert. On the outside of the box it said, "Do not eat if seal is broken." Of course . . . (these are third-grade jokes; try to keep up).

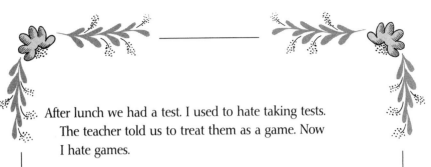

After lunch we had a test. I used to hate taking tests. The teacher told us to treat them as a game. Now I hate games.

I did get a 100 the other day, 50 in math and 50 in spelling.

My teacher is so forgetful she gave us the same test three weeks in a row. If she does that one more time, I might pass it.

My teacher knows all the answers! Of course she does—she makes up all the questions.

But I do better than my best friend, Mike. He made the PTA's Most Wanted list.

Mike's the biggest troublemaker in school. And his parents never thought he'd amount to anything!

When I get home from school, it takes me about an hour to do my homework—and two hours if my father helps.

I was having trouble in English. My dad bought me a cheap dictionary, but I couldn't find the words to thank him.

My dad bought me a thesaurus, too. I thought that was very nice, pleasurable, agreeable for him to do so.

I was doing geography homework, and I asked him where I would find the Catskills. He said, "I don't know, your mother puts everything away!"

When my father saw my report card, he said I was just like Abraham Lincoln. . . . I went down in history.

An Answer for Everything

Teacher: How old were you on your last birthday?
Student: Seven.
Teacher: How old will you be on your next birthday?
Student: Nine.
Teacher: That's impossible.
Student: No, it isn't, Teacher. I'm eight today.

Teacher: Tommy, why do you always get so dirty?
Tommy: Well, I'm a lot closer to the ground than you are.

Teacher: Willy, name one important thing we have today
that we didn't have ten years ago.
Willy: Me.

Mother: Why on earth did you
swallow that money I gave you?
Junior: You said it was my lunch money.

Teacher: How can you prevent diseases
caused by biting insects?
Jose: Don't bite any.

Sylvia: Dad, can you write in the dark?
Father: I think so. What do you want me to write?
Sylvia: Your name on this report card.

Teacher: In this box, I have a ten-foot snake.
Sammy: You can't fool me, Teacher. Snakes don't have
feet!

Teacher: Ellen, give me a sentence starting with "I."

Ellen: I is. . . .

Teacher: No, Ellen. Always say "I am."

Ellen: All right. I am the ninth letter of the alphabet.

Teacher: If I had seven oranges in one hand and eight oranges in the other, what would I have?

Class Clown: Big hands!

Behaving Like Angels?

A fourth-grade teacher had to leave the room for a few minutes. When she returned, she found the children in perfect order. Everyone was sitting absolutely quiet.

She was shocked and stunned and said, "I've never seen anything like it before. This is wonderful. But, please tell me, what came over all of you? Why are you so well-behaved and quiet?"

Finally, after much urging, little Sally spoke up and said, "Well, one time you said that if you ever came back and found us quiet, you would drop dead."

Card Catalog

Tommy found himself in a media center that still used the ancient card catalog system. He asked the librarian how to use the card catalog and she quickly explained.

After pouring over the little drawers full of cards, he approached the librarian again, wanting to know how to spell "tequila."

"T-e-q-u-i-l-a," said the librarian, and Tommy went back to his search.

A short time later he came to the desk, looking quite upset. "I just can't find it," he said.

"What book are you looking for?" the librarian asked.

"Tequila Mockingbird," said Tommy.

Circulation

A teacher was giving a lesson on circulation of the blood. Trying to make the matter clearer, he said, "Now class, if I stand on my head, the blood, as you know, would run into it, and I would turn red in the face."

"Yes, Sir," the class agreed.

"Then why is it that while I am standing upright in the ordinary position, the blood doesn't run into my feet?"

A fellow in the back shouted, "Cause your feet ain't empty!"

A Matter of Perspective

The children had all been photographed, and the teacher was trying to persuade them each to buy a copy of the group picture.

"Just think how nice it will be to look at it when you are all grown up and say, 'There's Jennifer—she's a lawyer now,' or 'That's Michael—he's a doctor.'"

A small voice at the back of the room rang out, "And there's the teacher. She's dead."

Map Reading

The teacher of the earth science class was lecturing on map reading.

After explaining about latitude, longitude, degrees, and minutes, the teacher asked, "Suppose I asked you to meet me for lunch at 23 degrees, 4 minutes north latitude, and 45 degrees, 15 minutes east longitude. . . . ?"

After a long silence, a voice volunteered, "I guess you'd be eating alone."

Kids' Science Quotes

One horsepower is the amount of energy it takes to drag a horse 500 feet in one second.

You can listen to thunder after lightning and tell how close you came to getting hit. If you don't hear it, you got hit, so never mind.

Talc is found on rocks and on babies.

The law of gravity says no fair jumping up without coming back down.

When people run around and around in circles, we say they are crazy. When planets do it, we say they are orbiting.

Rainbows are just to look at, not to really understand.

While Earth seems to be knowingly keeping its distance from the sun, it is really only centrificating. [This guy is going to do well in college!]

Someday we may discover how to make magnets that can point in any direction.

A vibration is a motion that cannot make up its mind which way it wants to go.

There are 26 vitamins in all, but some of the letters are yet to be discovered. Finding them all means living forever.

There is a tremendous weight pushing down on the center of Earth because of so much population stomping around up there these days.

Vacuums are nothings. We only mention them to let them know we know they're there.

Some oxygen molecules help fires burn while others help make water, so sometimes it's brother against brother.

Some people can tell what time it is by looking at the sun. But I have never been able to make out the numbers.

We say the cause of perfume disappearing is evaporation. Evaporation gets blamed for a lot of things people forget to put the top on.

In looking at a drop of water under a microscope, we find there are twice as many H's as O's.

I am not sure how clouds get formed. But the clouds know how to do it, and that is the important thing.

Clouds just keep circling Earth around and around. And around. There is not much else to do.

When they broke open molecules, they found they were only stuffed with atoms. But when they broke open atoms, they found them stuffed with explosions.

To most people, solutions mean finding the answers. But to chemists, solutions are things that are still all mixed up.

Legal Semantics

A teacher asked her class, "What is the difference between unlawful and illegal?"

Sammy quickly raised his hand.

"OK, answer, Sammy," said the teacher.

"Unlawful is when you do something the law doesn't allow and illegal is a sick eagle."

Lip Prints

According to a radio report, a middle school in Oregon was faced with a unique problem. A number of girls were beginning to use lipstick and would put it on in the bathroom. That was fine, but after they put on the lipstick, they would press their lips to the mirrors, leaving dozens of little lip prints. Finally, the principal decided that something had to be done.

She called all the girls to the bathroom and met them there with the custodian. She explained that all the lip prints were causing a major problem for the custodian, who had to clean the mirrors every day. To demonstrate how difficult this was, she asked the custodian to clean one of the mirrors. He proceeded to take out a long-handled brush, dip it into the toilet, and scrub the mirror.

There have been no more lip prints on the bathroom mirrors.

The Old Dog Trick

"Bobby, where's your homework?" Miss Martin sternly asked the little boy while holding out her hand.

"My dog ate it," was his solemn response.

"Bobby," answered Miss Martin, "I've been a teacher for 18 years. Do you really expect me to believe that?"

"It's true, Miss Martin, I swear," insisted the boy. "I had to force him, but he ate it!"

The Rest of the Story

A dad likes to read fairy tales to his two young sons at night. He has a good sense of humor and often ad-libs parts of the stories for fun.

One day, his youngest son's kindergarten teacher read the class the story of the Three Little Pigs. When she came to the part of the story where the first pig tries to get building materials for his home, she read, "...and so the pig went up to the man with a wheelbarrow full of straw and said, 'Pardon me, Sir, but might I have some of that straw so I can build a house?'" Then the teacher asked the class, "And what do you think that man said?"

My friend's son eagerly raised his hand and said, "I know! I know! He said, 'Holy smokes! A talking pig!'"

The teacher and students were in hysterics for the next ten minutes.

Sixth-Grade History Test

The following were answers provided by sixth-graders during a history test. Watch the spelling! Some of the best humor is in the misspelling. Even funnier–read aloud to someone else!

Ancient Egypt was inhabited by mummies and they all wrote in hydraulics. They lived in the Sarah Dessert. The climate of the Sarah is such that all the inhabitants have to live elsewhere.

Socrates was a famous Greek teacher who went around giving people advice. They killed him. Socrates died from an overdose of wedlock. After his death, his career suffered a dramatic decline.

Julius Caesar extinguished himself on the battlefields of Gaul. The Ides of March murdered him because they thought he was going to be made king. Dying, he gasped out: "Tee hee, Brutus."

Writing at the same time as Shakespeare was Miguel Cervantes. He wrote *Donkey Hote*. The next great author was John Milton. Milton wrote *Paradise Lost*. Then his wife died and he wrote *Paradise Regained*.

Beethoven wrote music even though he was deaf. He was so deaf he wrote loud music. He took long walks in the forest even when everyone was calling for him. Beethoven expired in 1827 and later died for this.

Johann Bach wrote a great many musical compositions and had a large number of children. In between he practiced on an old spinster which he kept up in his attic. Bach died from 1750 to the present. Bach was the most famous composer in the world and so was Handel. Handel was half German, half Italian, and half English. He was very large.

It was an age of great inventions and discoveries. Gutenberg invented removable type and the Bible. Another important invention was the circulation of blood. Sir Walter Raleigh is a historical figure because he invented cigarettes and started smoking. Sir Francis Drake circumcised the world with a 100-foot clipper.

Delegates from the original 13 states formed the Contented Congress. Thomas Jefferson, a Virgin, and Benjamin Franklin were two singers of the Declaration of Independence. Franklin discovered electricity by rubbing two cats backward and declared, "A horse divided against itself cannot stand." Franklin died in 1790 and is still dead.

Abraham Lincoln became America's greatest Precedent. Lincoln's mother died in infancy, and he was born in a log cabin which he built with his own hands. Abraham Lincoln freed the slaves by signing the Emasculation Proclamation. On the night of April 14, 1865, Lincoln went to the theater and got shot in his seat by one of the actors in a moving picture show. They believe the assinator was John Wilkes Booth, a supposingly insane actor. This ruined Booth's career.

More Sixth-Grade History

The nineteenth century was a time of a great
many thoughts and inventions. People
stopped reproducing by hand and
started reproducing by machine.

The invention of the steamboat
caused a network of rivers
to spring up.

Cyrus McCormick invented the McCormick
raper, which did the work of a hundred men.

Louis Pasteur discovered a cure for rabbits.

Charles Darwin was a naturalist who wrote the *Organ
of the Species*.

Madman Curie discovered the radio.

And Karl Marx became one of the Marx Brothers.

In the Olympic games, Greeks ran races, jumped,
hurled biscuits, and threw the java.

Joan of Arc was burnt to a steak and was canonized
by Bernard Shaw.

The Greeks were a highly sculptured people, and
without them we wouldn't have history. The Greeks
also had myths. A myth is a female moth.

Queen Elizabeth was the "Virgin Queen." As a queen
she was a success. When she exposed herself before
her troops they all shouted "hurrah."

New Spelling

Teacher: How do you spell "dog"?

Pupil: d, o, g, enter.

Urgent News From Jeffrey

Little Jeffrey wasn't getting good marks in school. One day he surprised the teacher with an announcement.

He tapped her on the shoulder and said: "I don't want to scare you, but my daddy says if I don't get better grades . . . somebody is going to get a spanking."

A Wise Schoolteacher

A wise schoolteacher sends this note to all parents on the first day of school: "If you promise not to believe everything your child says happens at school, I'll promise not to believe everything he says happens at home."

Who Said That?

As a fun assignment, a fourth-grade teacher gave her students the beginning of a list of famous sayings and asked them to provide an original ending for each one. Here are some examples of what they submitted:

The grass is always greener when you leave the sprinkler on.

• • •

The grass is always greener when you remember to water it.

• • •

If you can't stand the heat, go swimming.

• • •

A bird in the hand is a real mess.

• • •

No news is no newspaper.

• • •

A rolling stone plays the guitar.

• • •

To err is human, to eat a muskrat is not.

• • •

You have nothing to fear but homework.

• • •

It's always darkest just before you open your eyes.

• • •

If you can't stand the heat, don't start the fireplace.

• • •

A penny saved is nothing in the real world.

It's better to light one candle than to waste electricity.

· · ·

Better to light a candle than to light an explosive.

· · ·

The squeaky wheel gets annoying.

· · ·

We have nothing to fear but our principal.

· · ·

Laugh, and the world laughs with you. Cry, and
someone yells, "Shut up!"

· · ·

I think, therefore I get a headache.

· · ·

It's always darkest before 9:30 P.M.

· · ·

Early to bed and early to rise is first in the bathroom.

· · ·

A journey of a thousand miles begins with a blister.

· · ·

There is nothing new under the bed.

· · ·

Never put off 'till tomorrow what you should have done
yesterday.

· · ·

Don't count your chickens—it takes too long!

SAT Questions and Answers

These are supposedly answers that were given on a standardized test.

Question: Name 4 seasons.

Answer: Salt, pepper, mustard, and vinegar.

Question: Explain one of the processes by which water can be made safe to drink.

Answer: Flirtation makes water safe to drink because it removes the large pollutants like grit, sand, and dead sheep and canoeists.

Question: What is a planet?

Answer: A body of earth surrounded by sky.

Question: How is dew formed?

Answer: The sun shines down on the leaves and makes them perspire.

Wet Grades

A high school student came home from school seeming rather depressed.

"What's the matter, son?" asked his mother.

"Aw, gee," said the boy. "It's my grades. They're all wet."

"What do you mean 'all wet'?" asked the mother.

"I mean," he replied, "below C-level."

Political Correctness for Teenagers

No one fails a class anymore, he or she is merely . . .
   "passing impaired."

You don't have detention, you're just . . .
   "exit delayed."

Your bedroom isn't cluttered, it's . . .
   "passage restrictive."

These days, a student isn't lazy, he or she is . . .
   "energetically declined."

You're not sleeping in class, you're . . .
   "rationing consciousness."

No one's tall anymore, he or she is . . .
   "vertically enhanced."

You weren't passing notes in class, you were . . .
   "participating in the discreet exchange of penned
   meditations."

You're not shy, you're . . . "conversationally selective."

You don't talk a lot, you're just . . . "abundantly verbal."

You're not being sent to the principal's office, you're . . .
   "going on a mandatory field trip to the administrative
   area."

It's not called "gossip" anymore, it's . . . "the speedy
   transmission of near-factual information."

Analogies and Metaphors Found in High School Essays

Her face was a perfect oval, like a circle that had its two sides gently compressed by a Thigh Master.

. . .

His thoughts tumbled in his head, making and breaking alliances like socks in a dryer without Cling Free.

. . .

Her vocabulary was as bad as, like, whatever.

. . .

He was as tall as a six-foot-three-inch tree.

. . .

The little boat gently drifted across the pond exactly the way a bowling ball wouldn't.

. . .

Her hair glistened in the rain like a nose hair after a sneeze.

. . .

Even in his last years, Grandpa had a mind like a steel trap, only one that had been left out so long, it had rusted shut.

. . .

The young fighter had a hungry look, the kind you get from not eating for a while.

. . .

The ballerina rose gracefully and extended one slender leg behind her, like a dog at a fire hydrant.

college

College Application Essay

The following is an actual essay written by a college applicant. The author was accepted and is now attending the college that received this application.

In order for the admission staff of our college to get to know you, we ask that you answer the following questions: Are there any significant experiences you have had, or accomplishments you have realized, that have helped to define you as a person?

I am a dynamic figure, often seen scaling walls and crushing ice. I have been known to remodel train stations on my lunch breaks, making them more efficient in the area of heat retention. I translate ethnic slurs for Cuban refugees. I write award-winning operas. I manage time efficiently.

Occasionally, I tread water for three days in a row. I woo women with my sensuous and god-like trombone playing. I can pilot bicycles up severe inclines with unflagging speed, and I cook Thirty-Minute Brownies in twenty minutes. I am an expert in stucco, a veteran in love, and an outlaw in Peru.

Using only a hoe and a large glass of water, I once single-handedly defended a small village in the Amazon Basin from a horde of ferocious army ants. I play bluegrass cello, I was scouted by the Mets, I am the subject of numerous documentaries. When I'm bored, I build large suspension bridges in my yard. I enjoy urban hang gliding. On Wednesdays after school, I repair electrical appliances free of charge.

I am an abstract artist, a concrete analyst, and a ruthless bookie. Critics worldwide swoon over my original line

of corduroy evening wear. I don't perspire. I am a private citizen, yet I receive fan mail. I have been caller number nine and have won the weekend passes. Last summer I toured New Jersey with a traveling centrifugal-force demonstration. I bat .400.

My deft floral arrangements have earned me fame in international botany circles. Children trust me.

I can hurl tennis rackets at small moving objects with deadly accuracy. I once read *Paradise Lost, Moby Dick,* and *David Copperfield* in one day, and still had time to refurbish an entire dining room that evening.

I know the exact location of every food in the supermarket. I have performed several covert operations with the CIA. I sleep once a week, and when I do sleep, I sleep in a chair. While on vacation in Canada, I successfully negotiated with a group of terrorists who had seized a small bakery. The laws of physics do not apply to me.

I balance, I weave, I dodge, I frolic, and my bills are all paid. On weekends, to let off steam, I participate in full-contact origami. Years ago I discovered the meaning of life but forgot to write it down. I have made extraordinary four-course meals using only a toaster oven.

I breed prize-winning clams. I have won bullfights in San Juan, cliff-diving competitions in Sri Lanka, and spelling bees at the Kremlin. I have played Hamlet, I have performed open-heart surgery, and I have spoken with Elvis.

But I have not yet gone to college.

Asking for a Favor

Early in the semester, a student stops by during the professor's office hours. He bids her enter. She glances up and down the hall, steps in, closes the door, and says, "I would do anything to pass this class."

She steps closer to the desk, flips back her hair, and gazes meaningfully into his eyes. "I mean," she whispers, "I would do . . . anything."

The professor returns her gaze. "Anything?"

"Anything," she affirms.

The professor's voice drops to a whisper as he asks, "Would you . . . study?"

Laying Down Some Ground Rules

On the first day of college the dean addressed the students, pointing out some of the rules. "The female dormitory will be out-of-bounds for all male students, and the male dormitory to the female students. Anybody caught breaking this rule will be fined $20 the first time."

He continued, "Anybody caught breaking this rule the second time will be fined $60. Being caught a third time will incur a hefty fine of $180. Are there any questions?"

At that point, a male student in the crowd inquired, "How much for a season pass?"

Properties of Acids

During class, the chemistry professor was demonstrating the properties of various acids. "Now I'm dropping this silver coin into this glass of acid. Will it dissolve?"

"No, Sir," a student called out.

"No?" queried the professor. "Perhaps you can explain why the silver coin won't dissolve."

"Because," the student replied, "if it would, you wouldn't have dropped it in."

Learning About Observation

A lecturer teaching medicine was tutoring a class on "observation." He took out a jar of yellow-colored liquid. "This," he explained, "is urine. To be a doctor, you have to be observant to color, smell, sight, and taste."

After saying this, he dipped his finger into the jar and put it into his mouth. His class watched in amazement, most, in disgust. But being the good students that they were, the jar was passed, and one by one, they each dipped their finger into the jar and then put it into their mouths.

After the last student was done, the lecturer shook his head. "If any of you had been really observant, you would have noticed that I put my second finger into the jar and my third finger into my mouth."

Dreams and Aspirations

A school of agriculture's dean of admissions was interviewing a prospective student. "Why have you chosen this career?" he asked.

"I dream of making a million dollars in farming, like my father," the student replied.

"Your father made a million dollars in farming?" echoed the dean, much impressed.

"No," replied the applicant, "but he always dreamed of it."

Model Student

A college chemistry professor could not help but notice that one of his students was late to class for the third time that week. Before class ended, he went around the room asking students questions about the day's lecture. Of course, he made sure to pick on his tardy pupil.

"And who was it that discovered uranium?" the professor asked.

"I don't know," the student admitted.

"Perhaps if you came to class on time, Mr. Winters, you would know the answer," the professor admonished.

"That's not true," the student protested. "I never pay attention!"

Final Preparation

On the first day of class, the professor wished the students luck as he wrote a phone number on the blackboard. "If any of you have difficulty understanding the review material, call this number," he said as he dismissed class.

On Saturday afternoon, stumped by one of the review problems, a student reached for the phone, called the number, and heard a recorded message from Dial–a–Prayer.

Important Labels

A pharmacy major was taking a course in dispensing.

One day the class was discussing the various labels affixed to the prescription containers, such as "Take with food" and "Take with water."

The professor then distributed a few sample labels.

Days later he noticed that one member of the class had stuck one of them onto his chemistry textbook.

It read: "Caution: May cause extreme drowsiness."

One–Track Mind

The psychology instructor had just finished a lecture on mental health and was giving an oral test.

Speaking specifically of manic depression, the professor asked, "How would you diagnose a patient who walks back and forth screaming at the top of his lungs one minute, then sits in a chair weeping uncontrollably the next?"

A young man in the rear raised his hand and answered, "A basketball coach?"

Identifying Slogans

A professor was giving a lecture on company slogans in a college advertising and marketing class.

"Joe," he asked, "which company has the slogan, 'Come fly the friendly skies'?"

"United," Joe answered.

"Brenda, can you tell me which company has the slogan, 'Don't leave home without it'?"

Brenda answered the correct credit card company with no difficulty.

"Now, John, tell me who uses the slogan 'Just do it'?"

John thought for a moment, then answered, "My mom."

Final Exam

A professor stood before his class of 20 senior organic biology students, about to give out the final exam. "I want to say that it's been a pleasure teaching you this semester," he said. "I know you've all worked extremely hard and many of you are off to medical school after the summer. So that no one gets his or her GPA messed up because of too much celebrating this week, anyone who would like to opt out of the final exam today will receive a 'B' for the course."

There was much rejoicing among the class as students got up, thanked the professor, and signed out on his offer.

As the last taker left the room, the professor looked out over the handful of remaining students and asked, "Anyone else? This is your last chance." One more student accepted the offer.

The professor closed the door and took attendance of the remaining students. "I'm glad to see you believe in yourselves," he said. "You all have A's."

Reporting in From College

College student: "Hey, Dad! I've got great news for you!"

Father: "What, son?"

College student: "Remember that $500 you promised me if I made the Dean's list?"

Father: "I certainly do!"

College student: "Well, you get to keep it."

The Philosophy Final

A student taking a philosophy class had a single question on his final: "What is courage?"

The student wrote: "This," signed it, and turned it in.

Test Answers

A student is taking a true–false test and he's flipping a coin. At the end of the test he's flipping the coin again.

The teacher says, "What are you doing?"

He says, "Checking my answers."

Loaded Question

There were two sophomores who were taking an organic chemistry class. They did pretty well on all of the quizzes and the midterm, so they had solid A's going into the final.

These two friends were so confident about the final that they decided to party with some friends at another school upstate the weekend before finals week, even though the chemistry final was on Monday. They had a great time; however, with their hangovers and everything, they slept all day Sunday and didn't make it back to campus until early Monday morning.

Rather than take the final then, the two friends waited until the test was over, then went to find the professor to explain why they missed it. They told the professor that they'd gone out of town for the weekend and had planned to come back in time to study, but had a flat tire on the way back and didn't have a spare and couldn't get help for a long time, and so were late getting back.

The professor thought it over and agreed that they could make up the final the following day. The two friends were elated and relieved. They studied that night and went in to take the test the next day. The professor placed them in separate rooms, handed each of them a test booklet, and told them to begin.

The two students looked at the first problem, which was a simple one about free radical formation. It was worth 5 points. "Cool," they thought, "this is going to be easy!" They each completed the problem quickly and turned the page. They were unprepared, however, for what they found there: Which tire? (95 points)

The Stages of Students

At the start of college, the dean came in and said, "Good Morning," to the class. When they echoed back to him, he responded, "Ah, you're freshmen."

He explained . . .

When they say, "Good Morning," back, they're freshmen.

When they put their newspapers down and open their books, they're sophomores.

When they look up so they can see the instructor over the tops of the newspapers, they're juniors.

When they put their feet up on the desks and keep reading, they're seniors.

When they write it down, they're graduate students.

holidays

halloween

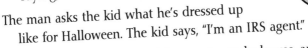

IRS Halloween

The doorbell rings, and a man answers it. Here stands this plain but well-dressed kid saying, "Trick or Treat!"

The man asks the kid what he's dressed up like for Halloween. The kid says, "I'm an IRS agent."

Then he takes 28 percent of the man's candy, leaves, and doesn't say, "Thank you."

A One-of-a-Kind Costume?

One Halloween, a trick-or-treater came to the door dressed as "Rocky" in boxing gloves and satin shorts.

Soon after I gave him some goodies, he returned for more.

"Aren't you the same 'Rocky' who left my doorstep several minutes ago?" I asked.

"Yes," he replied, "but now I'm the sequel. I'll be back five more times tonight."

Working Late on Halloween

Two men were walking home after a Halloween party and decided to take a shortcut through the cemetery.

Right in the middle of the cemetery they were startled by a tap–tap–tapping noise coming from the misty shadows.

Trembling with fear, they found an old man chipping away at one of the headstones with a hammer and chisel.

"Holy cow, Mister," one of them said after catching his breath. "You scared us half to death. We thought you were a ghost! What are you doing working here so late at night?"

"Those fools!" the old man grumbled. "They spelled my name wrong!"

Trick or Treat

At Halloween a couple had an unexpected guest. Instead of being home to greet trick–or–treaters, as they had planned to do, they went out with friends.

They hated to leave the house unattended and not give the numerous neighbor children any treats. So they set the bag of apples that they had intended to give out, on the porch with a sign that read: "Take some. Leave some."

When they got home later that night, they found three times as many apples as they had left for the trick–or–treaters.

A Dozen Ways to Confuse Trick-or-Treaters

1. Give away something other than candy (toothpicks, golf balls, bags of sand, etc.).

2. Wait behind the door. When they get near the door, jump out wearing a costume, holding a bag, and yell, "Trick or Treat!" Look at them, scratch your head, and act confused.

3. Get about 30 people to wait in your living room. When trick-or-treaters come to the door, invite them in. Once they're inside, have everyone yell, "Surprise!!!" Act like it's a surprise party.

4. After you give them candy, hand them a bill.

5. Open the door dressed as a giant fish. Collapse, flop around gasping for air, then don't move until they go away.

6. When you answer the door, hold up one candy bar, throw it out into the street, and yell, "Crawl for it!"

7. Hand out menus and let them order their candy. Keep asking if anyone wants to see the wine list.

8. Get a catapult. Sit on your porch and catapult pumpkins at anyone who comes within 50 yards of your house.

9. Answer the door dressed as a pilgrim. Stare for a moment, pretend to be confused, and start flipping through a calendar while mumbling "November."

10. Give away colored eggs instead of candy. If anyone protests, explain that you've been trying to get rid of the eggs since Easter.

11. Answer the door dressed as a dentist. Angrily lecture them about tooth decay until they leave.

12. When you open the door, shout, "Drop and give me twenty!" and insist they each do push-ups before you give them any candy.

thanksgiving

My Appetite Is My Shepherd

—Pound 23

My appetite is my shepherd; I always want.

It maketh me sit down and stuff myself.

It leadeth me to my refrigerator repeatedly.

It leadeth me in the path of Burger King for a Whopper.

It destroyeth my shape.

Yea, though I knoweth I gaineth, I will not stop eating

For the food tasteth so good.

The ice cream and the cookies, they comfort me.

When the table is spread before me, it exciteth me

For I knoweth that I sooneth shall dig in.

As I filleth my plate continuously,

My clothes runneth smaller.

Surely bulges and pudgies shall
   follow me all the days
   of my life

And I shall be "pleasingly
   plump" forever.

Missing Turkey

Ducking into confession with a turkey in his arms, Brian said, "Forgive me, Father, for I have sinned. I stole this turkey to feed my family. Would you take it and assuage my guilt?"

"Certainly not," said the priest. "As penance, you must return it to the one from whom you stole it."

"I tried," Brian sobbed, "but he refused. Oh, Father, what should I do?"

"If what you say is true, then it is all right for you to keep it for your family," the priest replied. Brian thanked him and hurried off.

When confession was over, the priest returned to his residence. When he walked into the kitchen, he found that someone had stolen his Thanksgiving turkey.

A Big Turkey

A lady was picking through the frozen turkeys at the grocery store, but she was unable to find one big enough for her family. She asked a stock clerk, "Do these turkeys get any bigger?"

He replied politely, "No Ma'am, they're as big as they're going to get. They're dead."

Gobble! Gobble! Gobble!

Q. What do you get when you cross a turkey with an octopus?
A. *Enough drumsticks for Thanksgiving*

Q. What kind of music did the Pilgrims like?
A. *Plymouth Rock*

Q. Which side of the turkey has the most feathers?
A. *The outside*

Q. Why did they let the turkey join the band?
A. *Because he had the drumsticks*

Q. Why did the police arrest the turkey?
A. *They suspected fowl play*

Turkey Surprise

The pro football team had just finished their daily practice session when a large turkey came strutting onto the field. While the players gazed in amazement, the turkey walked up to the head coach and demanded a tryout.

Everyone stared in silence as the turkey caught pass after pass and ran right through the defensive line.

When the turkey returned to the sidelines, the coach shouted, "You're terrific!! Sign up for the season, and I'll see to it that you get a huge bonus."

"Forget the bonus," the turkey said. "All I want to know is, Does the season go past Thanksgiving Day?"

Thanksgiving Forecast

Turkeys will thaw in the morning, then warm in the oven to an afternoon high near 190° F. The kitchen will turn hot and humid, and if you bother the cook, be ready for a severe squall or cold shoulder.

During the late afternoon and evening, the cold front of a knife will slice through the turkey, causing an accumulation of one to two inches on plates. Mashed potatoes will drift across one side while cranberry sauce creates slippery spots on the other. Please pass the gravy.

A weight watch and indigestion warning have been issued for the entire area, with increased stuffiness around the beltway. During the evening, the turkey will diminish and taper off to leftovers, dropping to a low of 34° F in the refrigerator.

Looking ahead to Friday and Saturday, high pressure to eat sandwiches will be established. Flurries of leftovers can be expected both days with a 50 percent chance of scattered soups late in the day. We expect a warming trend where soup develops. By early next week, eating pressure will be low as the only wish left will be the bone.

A Thanksgiving Poem

'Twas the night of Thanksgiving, but I just couldn't sleep.
I tried counting backwards; I tried counting sheep.
The leftovers beckoned—the dark meat and white,
But I fought the temptation with all of my might.
As I tossed and turned with anticipation,
The thought of a snack became infatuation.
So I raced to the kitchen, flung open the door,
And gazed at the fridge, full of goodies galore.
I gobbled up turkey and buttered potatoes,
Pickles and carrots and beans and tomatoes.
I felt myself swelling, so plump and so round,
'Til all of the sudden, I rose off the ground.
I crashed through the ceiling, floating into the sky
With a mouthful of pudding and a handful of pie.
But I managed to yell, as I soared past the trees,
"Happy eating to all—pass the cranberries, please!"

Thanksgiving Wishes

May your stuffing be tasty,
May your turkey be plump.
May your potatoes 'n gravy
Have nary a lump.
May your yams be delicious.
May your pies take the prize.
May your Thanksgiving dinner stay
Off of your thighs.

Top Ten Reasons Why College Students Are Looking Forward to Thanksgiving Break

10. Mother will not be serving mashed potatoes with an ice cream scooper.

9. You'll know that your turkey will be edible.

8. Pumpkin pie is a great alternative to green Jell-O.

7. After your eighth glass of cider, your emergency dash to the bathroom will not be delayed by having to line the seat with toilet paper.

6. Clean underwear, comfortable bed, access to a car, bedroom larger than an 8' x 10' cell . . . even if it is only for 4 days.

5. To eat your meals, the only trek you'll have to make is from the couch to the kitchen, rather than from the dorm to the dining hall . . . in below-freezing weather.

4. Instead of listening to "When I first started teaching here . . ." you can be entertained by "When I was your age . . ." or "During the Depression, we weren't lucky enough to have brussel sprouts. Hell, all we could afford was the sprout!"

3. You can eat your corn steamed with butter rather than popped in a microwave.

2. You won't be eating your Thanksgiving dinner off a tray!

1. You'll know that the hair in the shower drain is a DNA match to your own.

Christmas Dinner

A 4-year-old boy was asked to give the meal blessing before Christmas dinner. The family members bowed their heads in expectation.

He began his prayer by thanking God for all of his friends, naming them one by one. . . .

Then he thanked God for Mommy and Daddy, brother, sister, Grandma, Grandpa, and all his aunts and uncles. . . .

Then he began to thank God for the food. He gave thanks for the turkey, the dressing, the fruit salad, the cranberry sauce, the pies, and the cakes, even the Cool Whip.

Then he paused, and everyone waited—and waited. After a long silence, the young boy looked up at his mother and asked, "If I thank God for the broccoli, won't he know that I'm lying?"

Santa's Helpers

What do you call Santa's helpers?

Subordinate Clauses

Defying Physics

The professor was lecturing his physics class: "If molecules can be split into atoms and the atoms split into electrons, can the electrons be broken down any further?"

A student replied, "I'm not certain, but a sure way to find out would be to mail some of them in a Christmas package marked `Fragile'."

"Happy Holidays From . . ."

Rich and his wife had a hectic holiday schedule encompassing careers, teenagers, shopping, and all the required doings of the season. Running out of time, they got the stationer to print their signature on their Christmas cards instead of signing each one.

Soon they started getting cards from friends signed **"The Modest Morrisons," "The Clever Clarks,"** and **"The Successful Smiths."**

Then it hit them. They had mailed out a hundred cards neatly imprinted with **"Happy Holidays from the Rich Armstrongs."**

The Christmas Story

A little boy returned from Sunday school with a new perspective on the Christmas story. He had learned about the Wise Men from the East who brought gifts to the Baby Jesus. He was so excited that he just had to tell his parents.

"I learned in Sunday school today all about the very first Christmas! There wasn't a Santa Claus way back then, so these three skinny guys on camels had to deliver all the toys! And Rudolph the Red-Nosed Reindeer with his nose so bright wasn't there yet, so they had to have this big spotlight in the sky to find their way around!"

Away in a Manger

A mother was sitting with her 4-year-old son one night, sometime around Christmas. They were reading a book about the nativity story.

When they came to the part where Mary laid Baby Jesus in the manger, the mother said, "And here's the baby lyin' in the manger."

The son stopped for a moment and looked intently at the book. Then he turned to his mother with the most quizzical expression on his face and said, "But Mommy, where's the baby lion?"

Her Big Christmas Wish

The department store Santa Claus was more than a trifle surprised when a beautiful young lady about 20 years old walked up and sat on his lap.

But he quickly recovered and started talking to the college-type lass.

"And what do you want for Christmas?" asked Santa.

"Something for my mother," said the young lady.

"Well, that's what I call thoughtful," smiled Santa. "What can I bring for your mother?"

After a moment's thought, the girl brightened, turned to Santa, and said, "I'd like you to bring her a kind, caring, handsome, and all-around wonderful son-in-law."

The Gift of Harmony

"Thanks for the harmonica you gave me for Christmas," little Joshua said to his uncle, the first time he saw him after the holidays. "It's the best present I ever got."

"That's great," said his uncle. "Do you know how to play it?"

"Oh, I don't play it," the little fellow said. "My mom gives me a dollar a day not to play it during the day, and my dad gives me five dollars a week not to play it at night."

The Byte Before Christmas

'Twas the night before Christmas and all through the
house,
Not a user was using . . . not even a mouse.
The programs were hung from the bugs in their code,
In hopes that a guru would soon cure their woes.

The data were nestled all snug in their beds,
While versions of software danced in their heads.
The boss dimmed the lights as I locked up my desk,
A couple days off and a well-deserved rest.

Then all of a sudden there came such a clatter,
I sprang from my chair to see what was the matter.
Away to the processor I flew like a flash,
What a terrible sound . . . like a massive head crash.

The lights they were blinking and beaming aglow,
The hardcopy printout said, "Let service know!"
When what to my wandering eyes should appear,
On a silicon wafer . . . a field engineer;

A little device driver, so lively and quick,
I knew in a moment it must be St. Chip!
More rapid than Macro, his cursor insane,
He whistled and shouted like a video game.

Now, Pascal! Now, Basic! Now, Fortran and Cobol!
On RPG! On PL/1, on Dibol and Snobol!
To the top of the registers, the bottom of core,
Run diagnostics and see what they store!

As memory leaves when electricity flies,
The Rep cracked a smile and loosened his tie.
He was chubby and plump, said the place was a wreck,
And I laughed when I saw him (in spite of high tech).

A wink of his eye, and a twist of his head,
Soon let me know I had nothing to dread.
He was dressed from his head to his feet in a suit,
His briefcase was heavy with tools to re-boot.

With bundles of bits bulging out of his slacks,
He looked like a pro 'bout to fix a blown pack.
He spoke not a word, but went straight to his work,
Reseated PC boards, then turned with a smirk;

Hit enter with his finger and said, "Here it goes,"
And giving a nod, into the CRT he dove.
But I heard him exclaim, 'ere leaving the site,
"Restore the data, and all will be right!"

Christmas Eating Tips

It's easy to hate this time of year. Not for its crass commercialism and forced frivolity, but because it's the season when the Food Police come out with their wagging fingers and annual tips on how to get through the holidays without gaining ten pounds. You can't pick up a magazine without finding a list of holiday eating do's and donuts (oops, don'ts). Eliminate second helpings, high-calorie sauces, and cookies made with butter, they say. Fill up on vegetable sticks, they say. Good grief. Is your favorite childhood memory of Christmas a celery stick? A carrot was something you left for Rudolph. Here's a new list of tips for holiday eating:

1. About those carrot sticks. Avoid them. Anyone who puts carrots on a holiday buffet table knows nothing of the Christmas spirit. If you see carrots, leave immediately. Go next door where they're serving rum balls.

2. Drink as much eggnog as you can. And quickly. Like fine single-malt Scotch, it's rare. In fact, it's even rarer than single-malt Scotch. You don't find it any other time of year but now. So drink up! Who cares that it has 10,000 calories in every sip? It's not as though you're going to turn into an eggnogaholic or something. It's a treat. Enjoy it. Have one for me. Have two. It's later than you think. It's Christmas.

3. If something comes with gravy, use it. That's the whole point of gravy. Pour it on. Make a volcano out of your mashed potatoes. Fill it with gravy. Eat the volcano. Repeat.

4. As for mashed potatoes, always ask if they're made with skim milk or whole milk. If it's skim, pass.

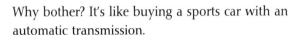

Why bother? It's like buying a sports car with an automatic transmission.

5. Do not have a snack before going to a party in an effort to control your eating. The whole point of going to a Christmas party is to eat other people's food for free. Lots of it. Hello.

6. Under no circumstances should you exercise between now and New Year's. You can do that in January when you have nothing else to do. This is the time for long naps, which you'll need after circling the buffet table while carrying a ten-pound plate of food and that vat of eggnog.

7. If you come across something really good at a buffet table, like frosted Christmas cookies in the shape and size of Santa, position yourself near them and don't budge. Have as many as you can before becoming the center of attention. They're like a beautiful pair of shoes. You can't leave them behind. You're not going to see them again.

8. Same for pies. Apple. Pecan. Pumpkin. Slice of each. Or, if you don't like pumpkin, have two apples and one pecan. Always have three. When else do you get to have more than one dessert? Labor Day?

9. Did someone mention fruitcake? Granted, it's loaded, but avoid it at all cost. I mean, have some standards, my dear.

10. And one final tip: If you don't feel terrible when you leave the party or get up from the table, you haven't been paying attention. Reread tips. Start over. But hurry! Cookieless January is just around the corner.

Ten Things to Say About a Christmas Gift You Don't Like

10. "Hey! There's a gift!"

9. "This is perfect for wearing around the basement."

8. "Boy, if I had not recently shot up four sizes, that would've fit."

7. "Well, well, well. . . ."

6. "Gosh, I hope this never catches fire! It is fire season, though—there are lots of unexplained fires."

5. "If the dog buries it, I'll be furious!"

4. "I love it—but I fear the jealousy it will inspire."

3. "Sadly, tomorrow I enter the Federal Witness Protection Program."

2. "To think—I get this gift the same year I vowed to give all my presents to charity."

1. "I really don't deserve this."

Ways to Confuse Santa Claus

- Instead of milk and cookies, leave him a salad and a note explaining that you think he could stand to lose a few pounds.
- While he's in your house, find his sleigh and write him a speeding ticket.
- Leave him a note explaining that you've gone away for the holidays. Ask if he would mind watering your plants.
- While he's in the house, replace all his reindeer with exact plastic replicas. Then wait and see what happens when he tries to get them to fly.
- Keep an angry bull in your living room. (If you think a bull goes crazy when he sees a little red cape, wait until he sees that big red Santa suit!)
- Leave a note by the telephone telling Santa that Mrs. Claus called to remind him to pick up some milk and a loaf of bread on his way home.
- Leave out a copy of your Christmas list with last-minute changes and corrections.
- Leave Santa a note explaining that you've moved. Include a map with unclear and hard-to-read directions to your new house.
- While he's on the roof, yell up to Santa and ask if he'd mind adjusting your satellite dish. When he does so, tell him, "That's good," and don't let him move until the commercials come on.

Holiday Parking Rules for Dingbats

It's that time again—the Holiday Shopping Season! So, for the dingbats out there, here's your list of parking rules. For the non-dingbats, be aware that the dingbats will be out in full force, and they'll be using the following rules:

Rule #1: When waiting for a parking spot, stop in the middle of the road, don't signal, and position your car diagonally to prevent others from passing.

Rule #2: Always park on the lines, taking up as many spots as possible. Diagonal parking is preferred.

Rule #3: In a crowded parking lot, if you find a spot and have the opportunity to pull through to an adjacent one, drive up halfway and stop on the line, taking both spots.

Rule #4: As you pull into a spot, if you see that the space ahead of you is empty and you see another driver signaling to take it, pull through and take it from him.

Rule #5: Always park close enough to the adjacent car so that the other driver must grease up with Vaseline to squeeze into his or her car.

Rule #6: When getting out of your car, hit the adjacent vehicle with your door really hard.

Rule #7: When driving through the parking lot, ignore the painted lanes and drive diagonally from one end to the other at a high rate of speed.

Rule #8: When stopped in front of a store to wait for a friend or relative to make a purchase, make sure you are stopped in the middle of the road. The same rule applies when picking up and discharging passengers. And don't use your emergency flasher—that's cheating.

Rule #9: When a vehicle from the opposite direction is signaling and waiting for a parking space, position your car so that you are in his way, and then let the car behind you take the spot.

Rule #10: If you have a disabled sticker, use a regular parking spot.

Kids Sing Christmas

No one can fracture a Christmas carol better than a child. Here's how some young folks completed lines to well-known Christmas carols. Sing along with these new takes on old favorites:

Deck the halls with Buddy Holly. . . .

We three kings of porridge and tar. . . .

On the first day of Christmas, my tulip gave to me. . . .

Later on we'll perspire, as we dream by the fire. . . .

He's makin' a list, chicken and rice. . . .

Frosty the Snowman is a ferret elf, I say. . . .

Sleep in heavenly peas. . . .

In the meadow we can build a snowman. . . .
    Then pretend that he is sparse and brown. . . .

Oh, what fun it is to ride with one horse, soap,
    and hay. . . .

Good tidings we bring to you and your kid. . . .

Noel, noel, noel, noel; Barney's the king of Israel. . . .

The Month After Christmas

'Twas the month after Christmas, and all through the house
Nothing would fit me, not even a blouse.
The cookies I'd nibbled, the eggnog I'd taste
At the holiday parties, had gone to my waist.

When I got on the scale there arose such a number!
When I walked to the store (less a walk than a lumber),
I'd remember the marvelous meals I'd prepared;
The gravies and sauces and beef nicely rared.

The cakes and the pies, the bread and the cheese
And the way I'd never said, "No thank you, please."
As I dressed myself in my husband's old shirt
And prepared once again to do battle with dirt.

I said to myself, as only I can,
"You can't spend the winter disguised as a man!"
So, away with the last of the sour cream dip;
Get rid of the fruitcake, every cracker and chip.

Every last bit of food I like must be banished
'Til all the additional ounces have vanished.
I won't have a cookie, not even a lick.
I'll only chew on a long celery stick.

I won't have hot biscuits, or corn bread, or pie,
I'll munch on a carrot and quietly cry.
I'm hungry, I'm lonesome, and life is a bore
But isn't that what January is for?

Unable to giggle, no longer a riot.
Happy New Year to all—and to all a good diet!

Politically Correct Santa

'Twas the night before Christmas and Santa was a wreck. . . .
How to live in a world that's politically correct?
His workers no longer would answer to "Elves";
"Vertically Challenged" they were calling themselves.

And labor conditions at the North Pole
Were alleged by the union to stifle the soul.
Four reindeer had vanished, without much propriety,
Released to the wild by the Humane Society.

And equal employment had made it quite clear
That Santa had better not use just reindeer.
So Dancer and Donner, Comet and Cupid,
Were replaced with four pigs, and you know that looked
    stupid!

The runners had been removed from his sleigh;
The ruts were termed dangerous by the E.P.A.
And people had started to call for the cops
When they heard sled noises on their rooftops.

Secondhand smoke from his pipe had his workers quite
    frightened.
His fur-trimmed red suit was called "Unenlightened."
And to show you the strangeness of life's ebbs and flows,
Rudolph was suing over unauthorized use of his nose

And had gone on The Tonight Show, in front of the nation,
Demanding millions in overdue compensation.
So, half of the reindeer were gone; and his wife,
Who suddenly said she'd enough of this life,

Joined a self-help group, packed, and left in a whiz,
Demanding from now on her title be "Ms."
And as for the gifts, why, he'd ne'er had a notion
That making a choice could cause so much commotion.

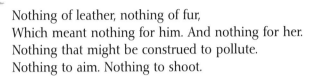

Nothing of leather, nothing of fur,
Which meant nothing for him. And nothing for her.
Nothing that might be construed to pollute.
Nothing to aim. Nothing to shoot.

Nothing that clamored or made lots of noise.
Nothing just for girls. Or just for the boys.
Nothing that claimed to be gender-specific.
Nothing that's warlike or non-pacific.

No candy or sweets . . . they were bad for the tooth.
Nothing that seemed to embellish a truth.
And fairy tales, while not yet forbidden,
Were like Barbie and Ken, better off hidden.

For they raised the hackles of those psychological
Who claimed the only good gift was one ecological.
No baseball, no football . . . someone could get hurt;
Besides, playing sports exposed kids to dirt.

Dolls were said to be sexist and should be passé;
And Nintendo would rot your entire brain away.
So Santa just stood there, disheveled, perplexed;
He just could not figure out what to do next.

He tried to be merry, tried to be gay,
But you've got to be careful with that word these days.
His sack was quite empty, limp to the ground;
Nothing fully acceptable was to be found.

Something special was needed, a gift that he might
Give to all without angering the left or the right.
A gift that would satisfy, with no indecision,
Each group of people, every religion;

Every ethnicity, every hue,
Everyone, everywhere . . . even you.
So here is that gift, its price beyond worth . . .
"May you and your loved ones enjoy Peace on Earth."

Some Assembly Required

'Twas the night before Christmas when all through
   the house,
I searched for the tools to hand to my spouse.
Instructions were studied and we were inspired,
In hopes we could manage "Some Assembly
   Required."

The children were quiet (not asleep) in their beds,
While Dad and I faced the evening with dread:
A kitchen, two bikes, Barbie's townhouse to boot!
And, thanks to Grandpa, a train to toot!

We opened the boxes, my heart skipped a beat. . . .
Let no pieces be missing or parts incomplete!
Too late for last-minute returns or replacement;
If we can't get it right, it goes down in the basement!

And what to my worrying eyes should appear,
But 50 sheets of directions, concise, but not clear,
With each part numbered and every slot named,
So if there were failure, only we could be blamed.

More rapid than eagles the parts then fell out,
And all over the carpet they were scattered about.
"Now bolt it. Now twist it! Attach it right there!
Slide on the seats, and staple the chair!

"Hammer the shelves, and nail to the stand."
"Honey," said hubby, "you just glued my hand."
And then in a twinkling, I knew for a fact
That all the toy dealers had indeed made a pact

To keep parents busy all Christmas Eve night
With "assembly required" 'till morning's first light.
We spoke not a word, but kept bent at our work,
'Til our eyes, they went bleary; our fingers all hurt.

The coffee went cold, and the night it wore thin
Before we attached the last rod and last pin.
Then laying the tools away in the chest,
We fell into bed for a well-deserved rest.

But I said to my husband just before I passed out,
"This will be the best Christmas, without a doubt.
Tomorrow we'll cheer, let the holiday ring,
And not have to run to the store for a thing!

"We did it! We did it! The toys are all set
For the perfect, most perfectest Christmas, I bet!"
Then off to dreamland, as last sweet repose
I gratefully went, although I suppose
There's something to say for those self-deluded;
I'd forgotten that BATTERIES are never included!

Four Stages of Life

1. You believe in Santa Claus.
2. You don't believe in Santa Claus.
3. You are Santa Claus.
4. You look like Santa Claus.

Some Assembly Required for Payment

A grandfather bought a hobby horse by mail order as a Christmas present for his granddaughter....

The toy arrived in 189 pieces!

The instructions said that it could be put together in an hour. However, it took the old man two days to assemble the toy.

Finally, when it was all put together, he wrote a check, cut it into 189 pieces, and mailed it off to the company.

New Year's Revisited

Do you ever have trouble keeping your New Year's resolutions? Here are a dozen suggestions for preventing the same situation from happening next year:

1. Gain weight (at least 30 pounds!).

2. Stop exercising. Waste of time.

3. Read less. Makes you think.

4. Watch more TV. You've been missing some good stuff.

5. Procrastinate more. Starting tomorrow.

6. Stop bringing lunch from home. Eat out more.

7. Get in a whole NEW rut!

8. Spend your summer vacation in cyberspace.

9. Eat cloned meat.

10. Get further in debt.

11. Don't believe politicians.

12. Never make New Year's resolutions again.

valentine's day

Valentine's Day (val en tinez dae)

- A day when you have dreams of a candlelight dinner, diamonds, and romance, but consider yourself lucky to get a card.

- A sign that the Web has affected your mind: You didn't give your valentine a card this year, but you posted one for your e-mail buddies on a Web page.

Her Valentine's Day Dream

After she woke up, a woman told her husband, "I just dreamed that you gave me a pearl necklace for Valentine's Day. What do you think it means?"

"You'll know tonight," he said.

That evening, the man came home with a small package and gave it to his wife. . . .

Delighted, she opened it to find a book entitled: **The Meaning of Dreams.**

Sending Valentine Cards

A woman walks into a post office one day to see a man standing at the counter methodically placing "Love" stamps on bright pink envelopes with hearts all over them. The man then takes out a perfume bottle and starts spraying all the envelopes. Her curiosity getting the better of her, she asks the man what he is doing. He says, "I'm sending out 1,000 Valentine cards signed, 'Guess who?'"

"But why?" asks the woman.

"Marketing—I'm a divorce lawyer."

A Very Special Day (Groundhog Day)

Over breakfast one morning, a woman said to her husband, "I bet you don't know what day this is."

"Of course I do," he answered indignantly, going out the door on the way to the office.

At 10:00 A.M., the doorbell rang, and when the woman opened the door, she was handed a box containing a dozen long-stemmed red roses.

At 1:00 P.M., a two-pound box of her favorite chocolates arrived.

Later, a boutique delivered a designer dress. The woman couldn't wait for her husband to come home.

"First the flowers, then the chocolate, and then the dress!" she exclaimed, throwing arms around him. "I've never had a more wonderful Groundhog Day in my whole life!"

st. patrick's day

A Lucky Clover

Patrick O'Reilly was lucky. Since the day he had found
that four-leaf clover, everything good seemed to come
his way. He had met the wonderful Rosie, and after a
whirlwind romance, they were married. And now, a
year later, he was the proud father of beautiful twins, a
boy and a girl.

At work, the story was the same. He had been promoted
and had received a substantial raise, and now the firm
had come up with a profit-sharing plan.

Paddy was certain his good fortune was due to his four-
leaf clover. Everywhere he went, he was certain to
be carrying the talisman in his suit pocket.

One morning Paddy could not find the clover. . . .

He searched the house, but it was not there. In panic,
he tried to recall when he had last seen it. He finally
recalled that it was in the gray suit he had dropped off
at the dry cleaners.

He rushed to the cleaners only to find that the work had
been done and his suit was ready to be picked up. He
searched the suit and found the four-leaf clover, still
in one piece but now flattened from the dry cleaning.

From that day on, Paddy's fortunes changed. Life was good, but no longer was it perfect. The little inconveniences were always there. . . .

He had a flat tire as he was driving to an important business meeting.

The twins came down with the flu when his boss and his wife were over for dinner.

Paddy's life had indeed changed. He still carried the amulet, but he was certainly not living under the silver lining he was used to and had come to expect.

Finally, he had had enough. He visited the parish priest to see if he could help him understand what had happened.

"This certainly was to be expected," the priest said. "You should have known—you should never press your luck."

Where Will I Put It All?!!!!

A man was standing in line at the bank when a commotion started at the counter.

A woman was distressed, exclaiming, "Where will I put my money?! I have all my money and mortgage here! What will happen to my mortgage?"

It turned out that she had misunderstood a small sign on the counter.

The sign read: WE WILL BE CLOSED FOR GOOD FRIDAY.

Free to Be Me

Memorial Day weekend was coming up, and the nursery school teacher took the opportunity to tell her class about patriotism.

"We live in a great country," she said. "One of the things we should be happy about is that, in this country, we are all free."

One little boy came walking up to her from the back of the room. He stood with his hands on his hips and said, "I'm not free."

The teacher quickly explained, "Even though your parents are always telling you what to do, it may seem to you that you are not free, but you truly are free."

The boy again said, "But I'm NOT free."

The teacher continued, "Yes, you really are free. Your parents just want you to grow up to be a well-behaved young man, so they work their hardest to give you the best values they possibly can."

The boy responded, "I'm not free. I'm four!"

**CORWIN
PRESS**

The Corwin Press logo—a raven striding across an open book—represents the union of courage and learning. Corwin Press is committed to improving education for all learners by publishing books and other professional development resources for those serving the field of PreK–12 education. By providing practical, hands-on materials, Corwin Press continues to carry out the promise of its motto: **"Helping Educators Do Their Work Better."**